When I Go Camping

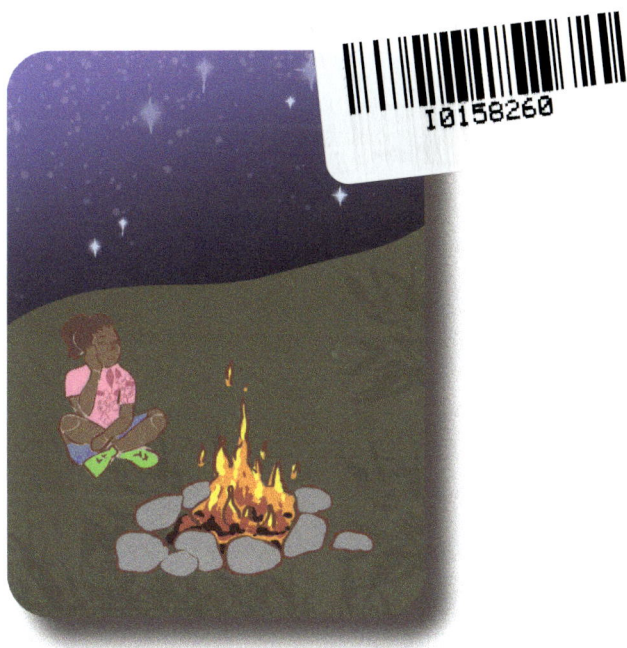

By Lateisha Bright

Illustrated by Kara Matters

Library For All Ltd.

Library For All is an Australian not for profit organisation with a mission to make knowledge accessible to all via an innovative digital library solution. Visit us at libraryforall.org

When I Go Camping

First published 2023

Published by Library For All Ltd
Email: info@libraryforall.org
URL: libraryforall.org

Our Yarning logo design by Jason Lee, Bidjipidji Art

Original illustrations by Kara Matters

When I Go Camping
Bright, Lateisha
ISBN: 978-1-923063-23-5
SKU03378

When I Go Camping

We respect and honour Aboriginal and Torres Strait Islander Elders past, present and future. We acknowledge the stories, traditions and living cultures of Aboriginal and Torres Strait Islander peoples on this land and commit to building a brighter future together.

43912

Every summer,
I go camping with
my family.

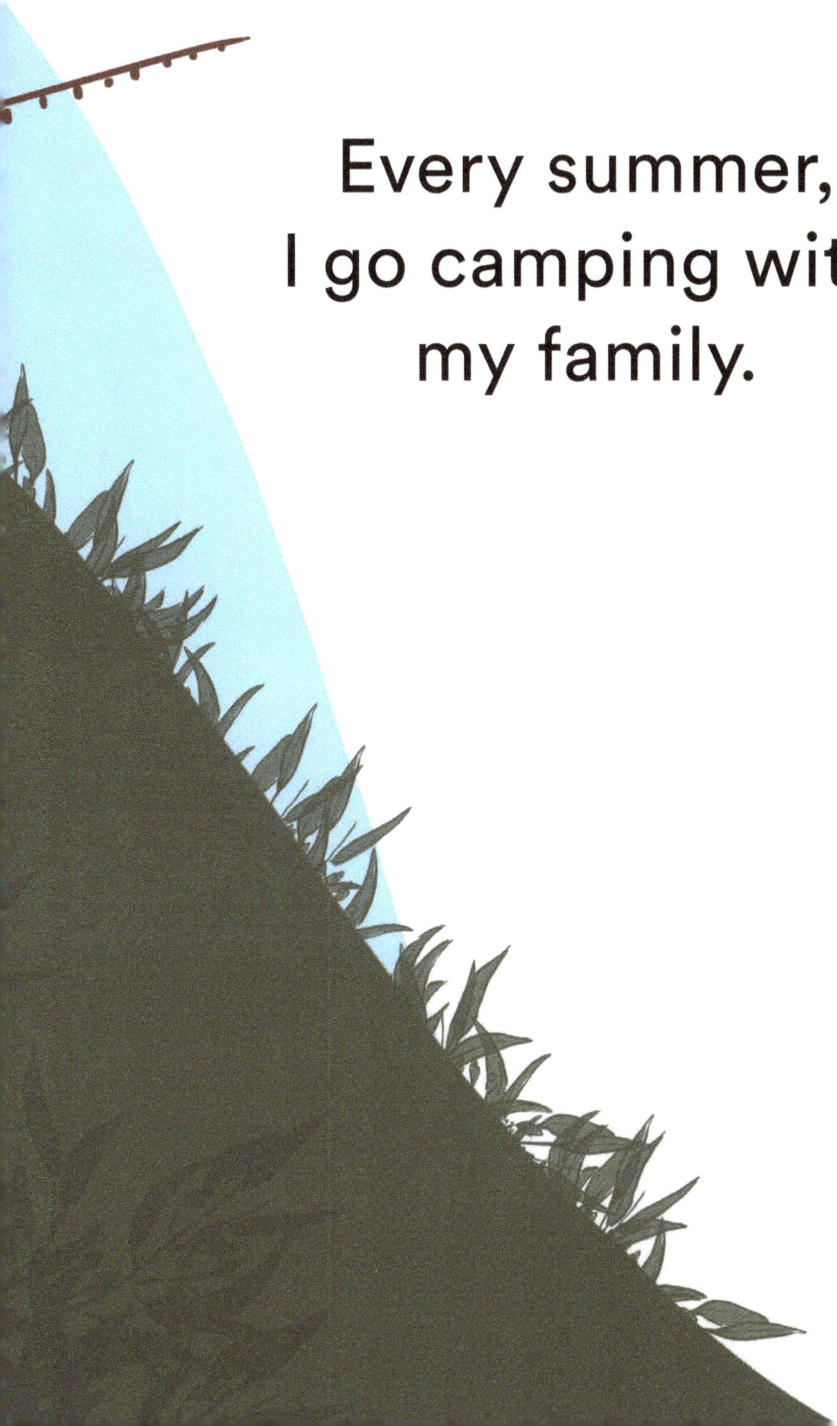

When I go camping,
I catch fish with
my nan.

When I go camping,
I swim in the river.

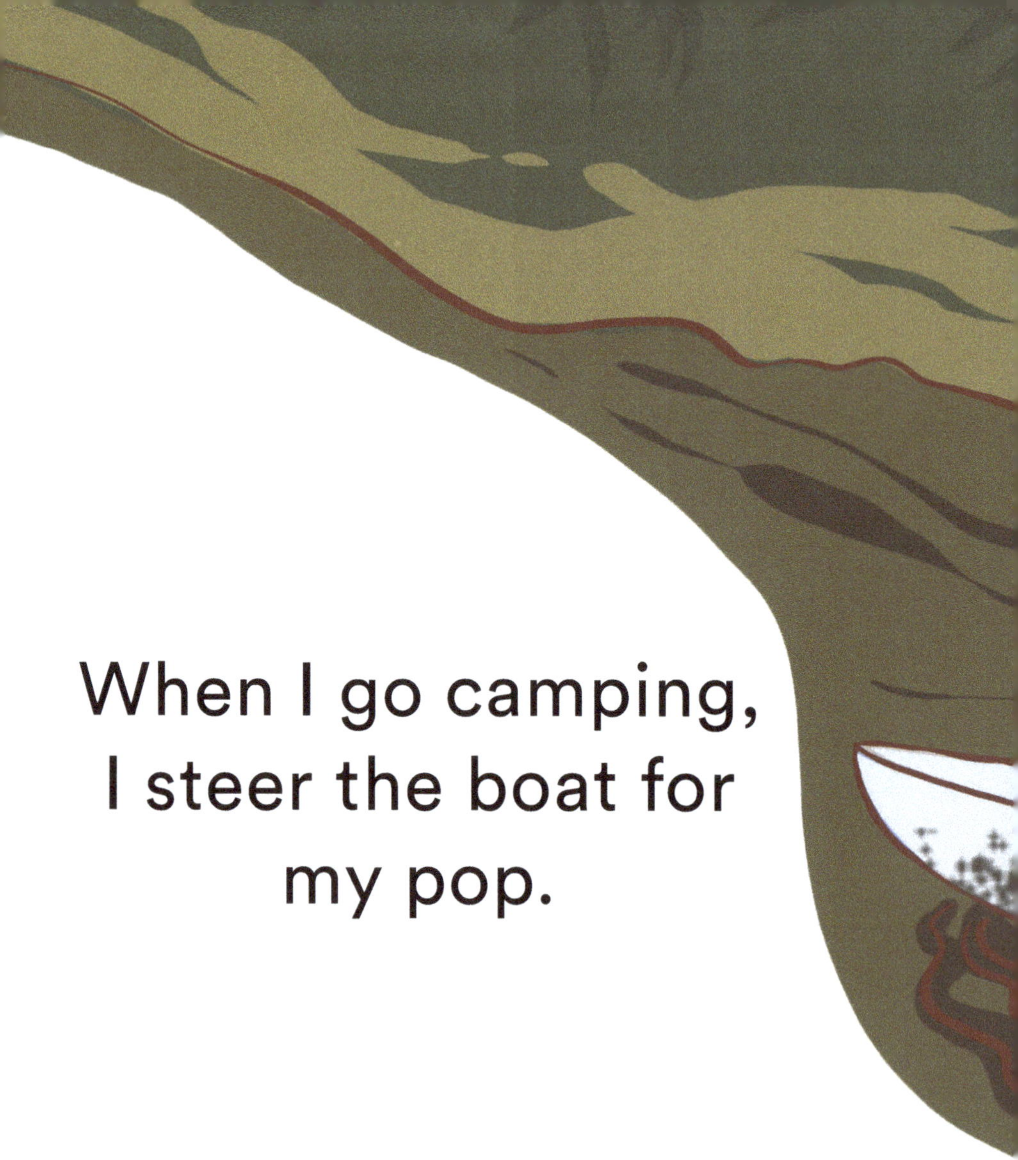

When I go camping,
I steer the boat for
my pop.

When I go camping,
I look for koalas in
the trees.

When I go camping,
I help cook fish on
the fire.

When I go camping,
I sleep in my swag.

When I go camping,
I gaze into the campfire.

When I go camping,
I am always happy.

What do you
do when you
go camping?

You can use these questions to talk about this book with your family, friends and teachers.

What did you learn from this book?

Describe this book in one word. Funny? Scary? Colourful? Interesting?

How did this book make you feel when you finished reading it?

What was your favourite part of this book?

download our reader app
getlibraryforall.org

About the contributors

Lateisha was born in Narrandera in New South Wales on Wiradjuri Country and now lives in Canberra on Ngunnawal Country. Lateisha loves to go camping with her family and fishing in the river. Her favourite story is *The Rainbow Serpent.*

Kara is a Noongar artist from Albany, Western Australia, with extensive experience in acrylic painting, digital art, illustration and design. Inspiration comes to Kara in all forms; she draws from the Earth, the Ocean, and what connects her emotionally to Country and soul.

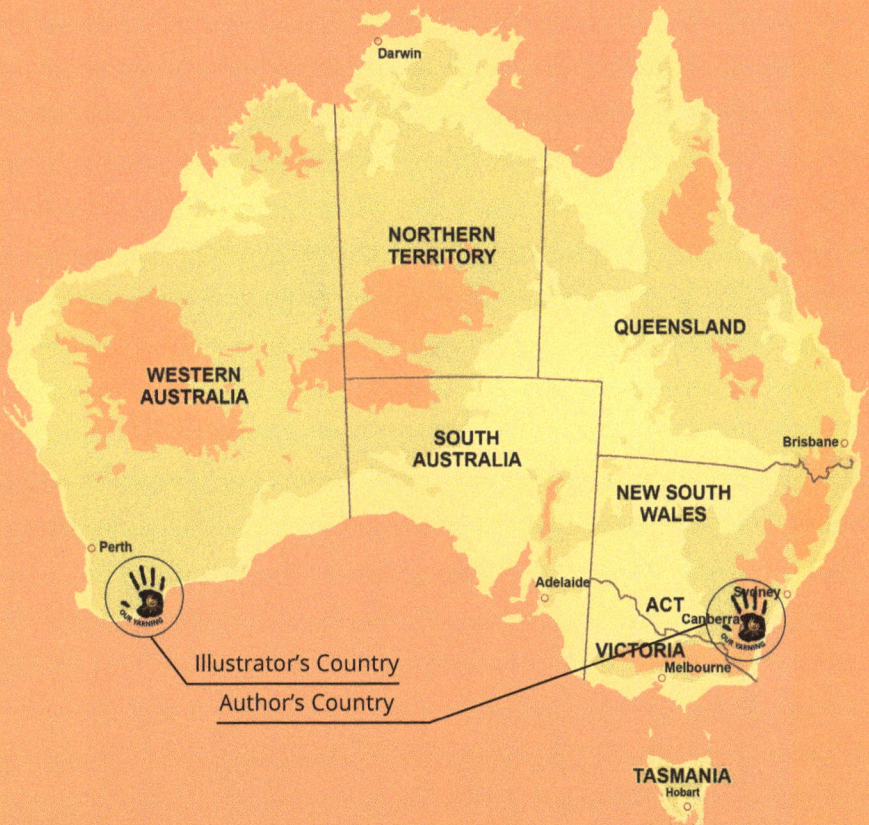

Darwin

NORTHERN TERRITORY

QUEENSLAND

WESTERN AUSTRALIA

SOUTH AUSTRALIA

Brisbane

NEW SOUTH WALES

Perth

Adelaide

ACT Canberra
Sydney

VICTORIA
Melbourne

Illustrator's Country
Author's Country

TASMANIA
Hobart

Our Yarning

Want to discover more books from this collection? Our Yarning is a collection of books written by Aboriginal and Torres Strait Islander peoples across Australia.

We know that children learn better, and enjoy reading more, when they see themselves in the stories, characters and illustrations of the books they read.

To download the app, visit the Google Play Store on any Android device and search 'Our Yarning'.

librariesforall.org